Primary 3A
Preface

Primary Mathematics Intensive Practice is a series of 12 books written to provide challenging supplementary material for Singapore's Primary Mathematics,

The primary objective of this series of books is to help students generate greater interest in mathematics and gain more confidence in solving mathematical problems. To achieve this, special features are incorporated in the series.

SPECIAL FEATURES

Topical Review
Enables students of mixed abilities to be exposed to a good variety of questions which are of varying levels of difficulty so as to help them develop a better understanding of mathematical concepts and their applications.

Mid-Year or End-Of-Year Review
Provides students with a good review that summarizes the topics learned in Primary Mathematics.

Take the Challenge!
Deepens students' mathematical concepts and helps develop their mathematical reasoning and higher-order thinking skills as they practice their problem-solving strategies.

More Challenging Problems
Stimulate students' interest through challenging and thought-provoking problems which encourage them to think critically and creatively as they apply their knowledge and experience in solving these problems.

Why this Series?
Students will find this series of books a good complement and supplement to the Primary Mathematics textbooks and workbooks. The comprehensive coverage certainly makes this series a valuable resource for teachers, parents and tutors.

It is hoped that the special features in this series of books will inspire and spur young people to achieve better mathematical competency and greater mathematics problem-solving skills.

Published by
SingaporeMath.com Inc
404 Beavercreek Road #225
Oregon City, OR 97045
U.S.A.
E-mail: customerservice@singaporemath.com
www.singaporemath.com

First published 2004
Reprinted 2005

ISBN 1-932906-04-5

Printed in Singapore

Our special thanks to Jenny Hoerst for her assistance in editing the
U.S. edition of Primary Mathematics Intensive Practice.

Primary 3A
Contents

Topic 1: Numbers to 10,000

1. Fill in the blanks in the table.

	Numeral	Thousands	Hundreds	Tens	Ones
(a)	8923	8		2	3
(b)	4706		7		6
(c)	2551	2			1
(d)	1848			4	

2. Look at the table above and fill in the blanks.

   (a) The numerals shown above are all _____-digit numbers.

   (b) Which numeral has 2 in the tens place? _____

   (c) Which digit in the numeral 4706 is in the thousands place?

   _____

   (d) In the numeral 1848, the digit _____ is in the hundreds place and the ones place.

   (e) In the numeral 2551, the digit 5 is in both the hundreds place and the _____ place.

3. Fill in the blanks.

   (a) 4578 = 4000 + 500 + 70 + _____

(b) 6045 = 6000 + _____ + 5

(c) 3629 = 3000 + _____ + 20 + 9

(d) 1730 = _____ + 700 + 30

(e) 4802 = 4000 + _____ + 2

(f) 9380 = 80 + 300 + _____.

4. Fill in the blanks.

   (a) In 4578, the digit '5' stands for _____.

   (b) The value of the digit '6' in the numeral 3629 is _____.

   (c) There are _____ hundreds in 6045.

   (d) In 2403, there are no _____ .

5. Complete this number sentence:

   9999 = 9000 + _____ + 90 + 9

6. (a) Which is the greater number, 6705 or 6805? _____

   (b) Which number is smaller, 1098 or 1089? _____

   (c) Which number is greater, 2081 or 2801? _____

   (d) Look at the four numbers below.

   3889, 6859, 3015, 4095

   The greatest number is _____.

   The smallest number is _____.

7. Arrange these numbers in order, starting from the smallest.

2916   2619   2069   2691

( )   ( )   ( )   ( )

8. Arrange these numbers in order, beginning with the greatest.

7843   8734   7438   8473

( )   ( )   ( )   ( )

9. Fill in the blanks.

(a) There are _____ tens in 460.

(b) There are _____ hundreds in 8600.

(c) 220 is the same as _____ tens.

(d) 5 tens more than 750 is _____.

(e) 2 hundreds less than 7033 is _____.

(f) 5260 is _____ more than 5000.

(g) 4123 is _____ less than 4153.

(h) 7066 is 100 more than _____.

(i) 3294 is 500 less than _____.

(j) The number that is 6 hundreds more than 2054 is _____.

(k) The number that is 4 thousands 4 tens less than 9182 is _____.

(l) There are _____ hundreds in 68 tens.

10. What is the missing numeral in each number pattern?

(a)

1688   2688   ⬭   4688

(b)

7965   ⬭   7765   7665

(c)

1979   1989   ⬭   2009   2019

(d)

5200   5230   5270   5320   ⬭

11. Fill in the blanks using the following digits.

7   0   8   4

(a) The greatest 4-digit number is _____.

(b) The smallest 4-digit number is _____.

(c) The greatest 3-digit number is _____.

(d) The smallest 3-digit number is _____.

12. Answer these questions.

(a) What is the largest 3-digit number?   _____

(b) What is the smallest 3-digit number?   _____

(c)   What is the answer if I subtract the smallest
      4-digit number from the   largest 4-digit
      number?   _____

13.   Fill in the blanks.

      (a)   The smallest 3-digit number comes just after _____.

      (b)   The largest 4-digit number comes just before _____.

      (c)   There are _____ numbers between 100 and 1000.

WORD PROBLEMS

1.   How much money total is 36 one-hundred dollar bills and 500 ten-
     dollar bills?

2. Shawn collected 1892 marbles. His classmate Gary collected 20 hundreds more. How many marbles did Gary collect?

3. There were 1688 spectators watching a football game. 50 tens of them were women and children and the rest were men. How many men were there at the game?

4. In a factory, workers pack candy into big cartons. Each big carton has:

   5 bags of 1000 pieces of candy each
   7 bags of 100 pieces of candy each
   8 bags of 10 pieces of candy each

   How many pieces of candy are there in one big carton?

5. At the end of a day, a bank teller counted all the money that she had collected as follows:

   3 one-thousand dollar bills
   9 one-hundred dollar bills
   24 ten dollar bills
   15 one dollar bills

   How much money had she collected for that day altogether?

6. If 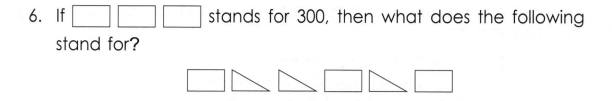 stands for 300, then what does the following stand for?

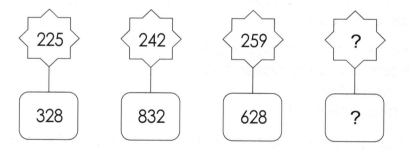

7. What are the missing numbers in the pattern below?

225	242	259	?
328	832	628	?

8. Thomas joins a very long line to collect tickets for the first showing of a new movie release. He is the 100th person from the first person in line. He is also the 100th person from the last one at the end of the line. How many people are in line?

9. Mrs. Lathan baked 3457 cookies for a bake sale. She packed them into as many large bags as possible of 100 each. She also packed some small bags of 10 each.

   (a) How many large bags and how many small bags did she pack?

   (b) How many cookies were left unpacked?

10. A shopkeeper sells marbles in boxes of 100s and bags of 10s. In a month, he sold 12 boxes and 338 bags of marbles. How many marbles were sold in that month?

Take the Challenge!

1. I am a three-digit number. All the three digits add up to 9. My tens digit is twice my hundreds digit and my ones digit is three times my tens digit. I have no zeros. Who am I?

2. I am a three-digit number. All the three digits add up to 13. My hundreds digit is three times my tens digit. My tens digit is three times my ones digit. What number am I?

3. In a train tunnel, signal lights are placed from the beginning to the end of the tunnel. The signal lights are spaced 20 m apart. There are altogether 6 signal lights. How long is the train tunnel?

1. Complete the following cross-number puzzle.

Across

(a)   589 + 2678

(b)   1693 + 1042

(c)   3814 + 1049

(d)   3085 + 2682

(e)   2548 + 2493

Down

(c)   7431 – 2909

(f)   9411 – 2895

(g)   5000 – 1627

(h)   10,000 – 4981

(j)   9254 – 1420

2. Find the sum.

(a) The sum of 594 and 1287 is _____.

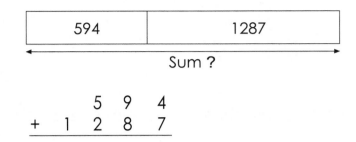

```
      5  9  4
+  1  2  8  7
_____
```

(b) The sum of 2395 and 1847 is _____.

(c) The sum of 1047, 318 and 789 is _____.

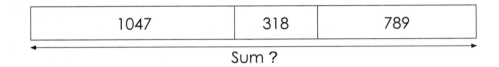

(d) The sum of 307, 2338 and 2166 is _____.

3. How many tens are there in the sum of 339 and 561? _____

4. How many hundreds are there in the sum of 2387 and 2813?

   _____

5. What is the sum of 8 thousands and 41 tens? _____

6. What is the sum of 8 hundreds 1 ones and 5 thousands 4 tens? _____

7. What is the number that is 149 greater than 17 hundreds?

_____

17 hundreds	149

?

8. What number is greater than 46 tens by 5054? _____

9. Find the difference.

   (a) The difference between 9753 and 2461 is _____.

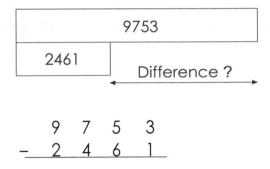

	9753
2461	

Difference ?

```
    9 7 5 3
  - 2 4 6 1
```

   (b) The difference between 8257 and 1356 is _____.

(c) The difference between the greatest and the smallest of three numbers 5047, 3278 and 1318 is _____.

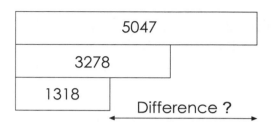

(d) The difference between the largest and the smallest of three numbers 1276, 629 and 5687 is _____.

10. What is the difference between 11 hundreds and 42 tens?

_____

11. What is the difference between 247 tens and 1 thousand 64 ones? _____

12. What is the number that is 1409 less than 8023? _____

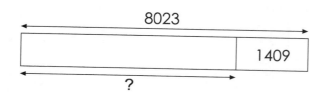

13. What number is smaller than 4 thousands 32 ones by 154 tens? _____

14. What is the missing digit in each box?

(a)
```
    5  8  9
 +  ☐  8  7
 ─────────
    9  ☐  6
 ─────────
```

(b)
```
    3  8  5
 +  1  6  ☐  7
 ───────────
    2  ☐  8  2
 ───────────
```

(c)
```
    7  5  ☐  3
 −  2  6  7  8
 ────────────
    ☐  8  2  5
 ────────────
```

(d)
```
    7  4  2
 −  ☐  8  9
 ──────────
    1  ☐  3
 ──────────
```

(e)
```
    7 0 5 3
  -  1 6 □ 7
  _____
    □ 3 8 6
```

(f)
```
    2 5 3 □
  + 2 9 7 8
  _____
    5 □ 1 7
```

15. Using each of the digits 3, 0, 8 and 6 only once, form the greatest

number. _____

16. Using each of the digits 5, 9, 1 and 4 only once, form the smallest

number. _____

17. Subtract 3562 from 10,000. What is the value of the digit '4' in your

answer? _____

18. Add 2780 to 1232. Which digit is in the hundreds place? _____

18

19. When I add two numbers together, they give a sum of 2312. If one of the numbers is 859, what is the other number? _____

20. What is the number I must add to the sum of 312 and 338 to get 800? _____

21. What number must be added to the difference between 312 and 452 to get 200? _____

22. A number is less than a second number by 279. The smaller number is 758. What is the larger number? _____

23. The difference between two numbers is 176. If the larger number is 1164, find the smaller number. _____

24. The sum of three numbers is 9999. Two of the numbers are 2001 and 1997. What is the third number? _____

25. The sum of two numbers is 100. The smaller number is 60 less than the bigger number. What is the smaller number? _____

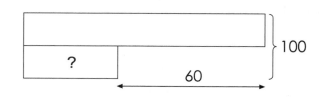

26. The sum of two numbers is 1000. The difference between them is 400. Find the larger number. _____

WORD PROBLEMS

1. Sarah gave 217 beads to Jenny and had 198 left. How many beads did Sarah have at first?

2. Joshua had 136 more picture cards than Samuel. If Samuel had 98 picture cards, how many picture cards did the two boys have?

3. A train left Orchard Station with 919 passengers. At the next station, 468 passengers got off the train and another 789 passengers got on the train. How many passengers were on the train then?

4. (a) Form the largest 4-digit number and the smallest 4-digit number using each of these digits only once.

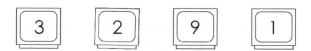

(b) What is the difference between these two numbers?

5. What is the sum of the greatest 4-digit number and the smallest 4-digit number that can be formed using all of the following digits?

6. Clarissa counted 1234 colored bubbles on a drawing. 123 were blue, 234 were yellow, 345 were red and the rest were green. Can you help Clarissa find out the number of green bubbles?

7. Mr. Postman delivered 2244 letters in the morning. He delivered 750 fewer letters in the afternoon. How many letters did Mr. Postman deliver a day?

8. 9 thousand people attended a concert. There were 1489 adults, 3625 boys and the rest were girls.

   (a) How many girls attended the concert?

   (b) How many more boys and girls than adults were there?

9. There are 500 beads. They are put into 3 jars. The first jar contains 275 beads and the third jar contains only 79 beads. How many beads are put into the second jar?

10. Winnie collected 2400 coins. She gave 1675 coins to a friend and kept the rest. If Winnie again collected the same number of coins she kept, how many coins would she have in the end?

Take the Challenge!

1. Put the digits 2, 3, 4, 5, 6 and 7 into the boxes below to form two 3-digit numbers that add up to 603. One of the 3-digit numbers is even while the other is odd.

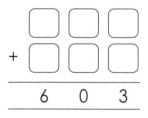

2. I have 300 gold and silver star stickers. The number of silver star stickers is twice the number of gold star stickers. I gave away 45 silver star stickers. How many more silver star stickers than gold star stickers do I still have?

3. What number does each of the letters stand for?

```
        E   A
  +     E   A
  _____
    K   A   A
```

4. What do the letters A, B, C and D stand for such that both the addition sums are true? (A, B, C and D stand for different single-digit numbers.)

```
      A   B                    C   B
  +   C   D                +   A   D
  _____         _____
    1   0   0                1   0   0
```

Topic 3: Multiplication and Division
by 2, 3, 4, 5 and 10

1. Fill in the missing number or numbers in each number sequence.

(a) (6) (9) ( ) (15) (18)

(b) (8) (10) (12) ( ) (16)

(c) (25) ( ) (35) (40) (45)

(d) (40) (50) ( ) (70) (80)

(e) (16) (20) (24) ( ) (32)

(f)

5	25			50	
1	5	9	6	10	7

(g)

8 → 24   7 →   4 → 12   9 →

28

(h)

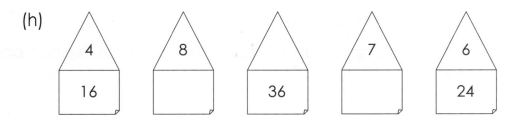

2. Study the number patterns and fill in the missing numbers.

(a)

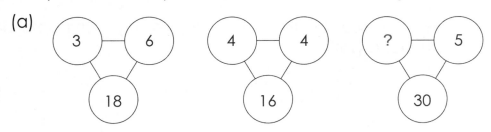

(b)

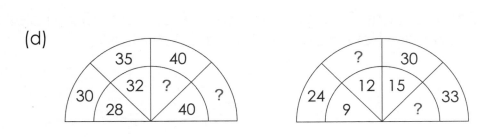

(c)

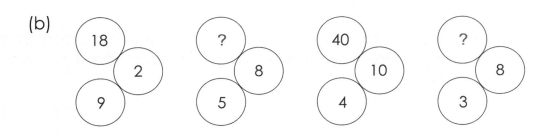

(d)

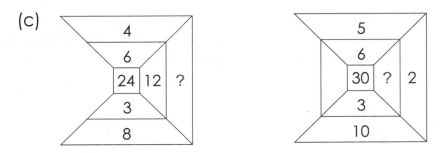

3. Write out the number sentence.

(a) I bought 4 bags of apples. There are 5 apples in each bag. How many apples did I buy?

$$\boxed{} \bigcirc \boxed{} = \boxed{}$$

(b) 5 friends share 45 storybooks. How many storybooks does each friend get?

$$\boxed{} \bigcirc \boxed{} = \boxed{}$$

(c) Mr. Thompson has 3 mini-vans. Each mini-van can carry 9 passengers. How many passengers can the 3 mini-vans carry?

$$\boxed{} \bigcirc \boxed{} = \boxed{}$$

(d) Mrs. Ling put 36 pots of orchids equally in 4 rows. How many pots of orchids did she put in a row?

$$\boxed{} \bigcirc \boxed{} = \boxed{}$$

(e) Peter bought 5 bags of marbles. There are 10 marbles in each bag. How many marbles did Peter buy?

$$\boxed{} \bigcirc \boxed{} = \boxed{}$$

(f) Mary has 5 bags of candy. She has 35 pieces of candy altogether. How many pieces of candy are there in each bag?

$$\boxed{} \bigcirc \boxed{} = \boxed{}$$

4. Use model drawings to help you in the following questions.

Example: Ravi has 3 times as many animal cards as plant cards. He has 8 plant cards. How many animal cards does he have?

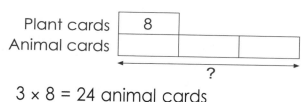

3 x 8 = 24 animal cards

(a) Ned ate 3 times as many cherries as his brother. If his brother ate 5 cherries, how many cherries did Ned eat?

(b) James had 4 times as many toy cars as Ryan. If James had 32 toy cars, how many toy cars did Ryan have?

(c) Christina collected 40 stamps. She collected 5 times as many stamps as Britney. How many stamps did Britney collect?

(d) Buffy can complete 4 pages of a math workbook in 1 day. How many pages of the workbook can she complete in 1 week? (There are 7 days in a week.)

5. Find the product of these numbers.

(a)
```
     7 6
  ×    3
  ──────

  ──────
```

(b)
```
     4 8
  ×    4
  ──────

  ──────
```

(c)
```
     8 9
  ×    5
  ──────

  ──────
```

(d)
```
   1 0 0
  ×    5
  ──────

  ──────
```

(e)
```
   3 5 0
  ×    3
  ──────

  ──────
```

(f)
```
   7 0 0
  ×    4
  ──────

  ──────
```

(g)
```
   9 3 8
  ×    4
  ──────

  ──────
```

(h)
```
   6 1 9
  ×    2
  ──────

  ──────
```

(i)
```
   7 6 5
  ×    3
  ──────

  ──────
```

(j)   6 9 2   (k)   2 5 8   (l)   4 0 9
    ×   4   ×   5   ×   3
    _____   _____   _____

    _____   _____   _____

6. Divide and find the quotient and remainder of each of the following.

(a)   (b)   (c)
    2) 5 5   5) 1 1 1   4) 2 0 5

(d)   (e)   (f)
    3) 6 8   4) 4 3 7   5) 6 6 3

(g)   (h)   (i)
    4) 3 7 8   2) 4 5 0   3) 3 5 9

(j)   (k)   (l)
    5) 8 0 8   3) 4 6 1   4) 9 0 2

7. If ✧ ✧ ✧ stands for 27 stickers, then

✧ ✧ ✧ ✧ ✧ stands for _____ stickers.

8. If ✦ + ✦ + ✦ + ✦ + ✦ = 30,

then ✦ + ✦ + ✦ = _____ .

9. How many fives are there in 295? _____

10. How many fours are there in 948? _____

11. If 24 ÷ ♡ = ☆ and ♡ = 4, then ☆ × ☆ × ♡ = _____ .

12. If ◇ + ◇ + ◇ gives 123
    and ◹ + ◹ + ◹ + ◹ gives 20, what is the product of
    ◇ and ◹ ? _____

34

13. $\boxed{} \times 4 = 672$

   What is the missing number in the box? _____

14. $\boxed{} \div 5 = 483$

   What is the missing number in the box? _____

15. Fanny is counting in fours. She made a mistake in one of the sets. Which one is it? Put a cross in the box next to it.

   32, 36, 40, 44 $\boxed{}$

   48, 52, 56, 61 $\boxed{}$

16. What is the remainder when you divide 431 by 5? _____

17. What number gives a quotient of 45 and a remainder of 2 when it is divided by 4? _____

18. Divide 420 by 5. The answer is the same as the product of 21 and
_____ .

19. How many times can you subtract 5 from 201? _____

20. Fill in the missing number in each box below.

(a)
```
    3 ☐ 8
  ×     4
  ─────────
  1 4 7 2
  ─────────
```

(b)
```
        1 3 2
  ☐ ) 3 9 6
```

21. What is the digit in each box?

(a)
```
      1 6 r2
  5 ) 8 ☐
```

(b)
```
      7 2 ☐
  ×       5
  ─────────
    3 6 4 5
  ─────────
```

WORD PROBLEMS

1. One car has 4 wheels. How many wheels do 48 cars have?

2. Ronnie sells 128 cakes each week. How many cakes will he sell in 10 weeks?

3. A farmer plants 185 apple trees in 1 plot of land. How many apple trees can he plant if he has 5 plots of land?

4. Mr. Lim had 203 books. He sold 75 of them and placed the rest of the books equally into 4 boxes. How many books are there in 1 box?

5. Davina can only fill each page of her sticker album with 36 stickers. She fills 3 pages and has 12 stickers left over. How many stickers does Davina have in all?

6. Aaron has twice the number of guppies as swordtails in his aquarium. He has 43 swordtails. How many more guppies than swordtails does Aaron have?

7. Sam has 198 cards. Juan has twice as many cards as Sam. How many cards do Sam and Juan have?

8. Casey has 3 times as many coins as Marty. How many coins do both of them have if Marty has 687?

9. A grocer bought 782 lollipops. She packed them into bags of 3 each.
   (a) How many bags did she get?
   (b) How many lollipops were left over?

10. Billie has 15 marbles. Millie has 3 times as many marbles as Billie. How many more marbles does Millie have?

Take the Challenge!

1. I thought of a certain number.
   I have forgotten what this number is.
   Can you help me to find out what it is?

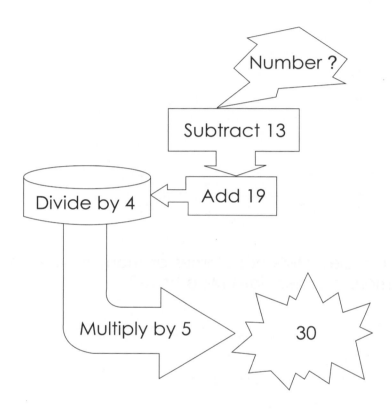

2. Abigail is 12 years older than her sister Davinia. How old will Davinia be when Abigail is 3 times as old as she is?
(*Hint*: The difference in age is always the same at any time.)

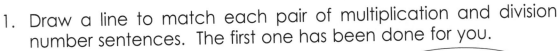

Topic 4: Multiplication and Division by 6, 7, 8, and 9

1. Draw a line to match each pair of multiplication and division number sentences. The first one has been done for you.

(a) 6 × 6 = 36

(b) 8 × 6 = 48

(c) 5 × 9 = 45

(d) 8 × 7 = 56

(e) 9 × 8 = 72

(f) 6 × 9 = 54

(g) 7 × 9 = 63

(h) 6 × 7 = 42

45 ÷ 5 = 9

56 ÷ 7 = 8

63 ÷ 7 = 9

36 ÷ 6 = 6

54 ÷ 9 = 6

42 ÷ 7 = 6

48 ÷ 8 = 6

72 ÷ 8 = 9

2. Study each number pattern and fill in the missing numbers.

(a)

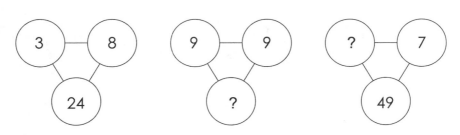

(b)

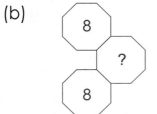 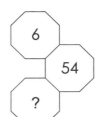 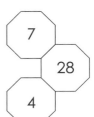

(c)

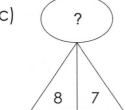 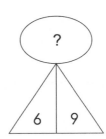

(d)

5	1
20	4

3	2
24	16

3	7
18	?

(e)

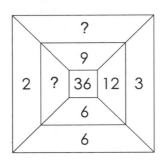 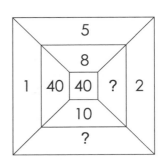

3. Find the product of these numbers.

(a)
```
    1 0 6
  ×     7
  _____

  _____
```

(b)
```
    2 8 5
  ×     6
  _____

  _____
```

(c)
```
    3 9 2
  ×     8
  _____

  _____
```

(d)
```
    6 8 7
  ×     9
  _____

  _____
```

(e)
```
    3 1 4
  ×     7
  _____

  _____
```

(f)
```
    7 5 0
  ×     8
  _____

  _____
```

(g)
```
    5 9 4
  ×     6
  _____

  _____
```

(h)
```
    2 8 9
  ×     9
  _____

  _____
```

(i)
```
    4 8 5
  ×     6
  _____

  _____
```

(j)
```
    2 8 3
  ×     8
  _____

  _____
```

(k)
```
    7 0 4
  ×     7
  _____

  _____
```

(l)
```
    4 0 9
  ×     9
  _____

  _____
```

4. Divide each of the following.

(a)
```
  6) 8 5
```

(b)
```
  7) 9 3 4
```

(c)
```
  8) 5 0 4
```

(d)

$9\overline{)677}$

(e)

$8\overline{)895}$

(f)

$7\overline{)664}$

(g)

$6\overline{)398}$

(h)

$9\overline{)454}$

(i)

$8\overline{)457}$

(j)

$7\overline{)909}$

(k)

$6\overline{)394}$

(l)

$8\overline{)999}$

5. Use model drawings to help you in the following questions.
   Example: 625 mandarin oranges are packed equally into 7 boxes.
   How many mandarin oranges are there in 1 box? How
   many oranges cannot be packed into a box?

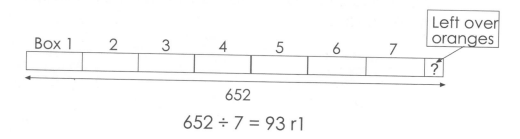

$652 \div 7 = 93 \text{ r1}$

There are 93 oranges in 1 box.
1 orange cannot be packed into a box.

(a) Aaron ordered 8 boxes of honeydews. There were 2 dozen honeydews in each box. How many honeydews did he have? (1 dozen = 12)

(b) 10 jars of the same type contain 350 cookies. How many cookies do 6 such jars contain?

(c) Peter has 9 stamp albums. Each album contains 352 stamps. If Peter gives 512 stamps to his borther, how many stamps does he have left?

6. ☐ × 6 = 772 ÷ 8

What is the missing number in the box? _____

7. 992 ÷ 8 = 31 × ☐

What is the missing number in the box? _____

8. Jonathan is counting in steps of 7. He made a mistake in one of the sets. Which one is it? Put a cross in the box next to it.

     21,   28,   35,   43   ☐

     49,   56,   63   70   ☐

9. What is the next number? _____

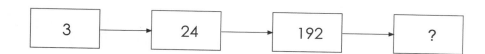

| 3 | → | 24 | → | 192 | → | ? |

10. I have a certain number. When I divide the number by 9, it becomes 82 and has a remainder of 4. What is the number? _____

11. If 7 × 205 = 1435, without using multiplication, what is 8 × 205?

_____

12. If [notepads image] stands for 972 notepads,

[notepads image] stands for _____ notepads.

13. The product of _____ and 69 is 483.

14. Fill in the missing number in each box below.

(a)
```
      8 □ 3
    ×     9
    ───────
    7 5 8 7
    ───────
```

(b)
```
              6  8  r2
            ──────────
        □ ) 5  4  6
```

15. What is the missing digit in each box?

(a)
```
          1  3  6  r6
        ─────────────
      7 ) 9  □  8
```

(b)
```
        7  8  9
    ×         □
    ───────────
    4  7  3  4
    ───────────
```

16. Study each pattern below and fill in the missing number.

(a)

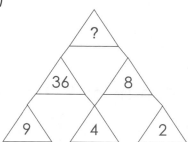

(b)

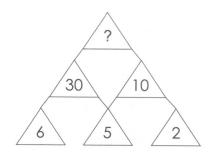

50

17. Joel was supposed to multiply a number by 7, but by mistake he divided the number. The answer he obtained was 49. Can you help Joel work out the correct answer?

WORD PROBLEMS

1. The number of pages in one book is 464. This is 8 times the number of pages in another book. How many pages are there in the other book?

2. Monica and Vivien shared 400 coins. Monica received 7 times as many coins as Vivien. How many coins did Monica receive?

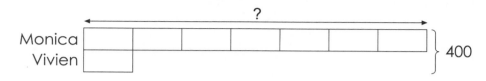

3. A carton contains 10 bowls and 6 plates. Amy needs 138 plates for her new restaurant.
   (a) How many cartons must she buy?
   (b) How many bowls did she also get?

4. Albert arranged 8 chairs in a row in a hall. There were 45 chairs in each column. How many chairs must Albert arrange for 2 such halls?

5. Mrs. Wright prepared 9 tins for the cookies she baked. She packed 238 cookies into each tin after throwing away 27 burned ones. How many cookies did she bake at first?

6. A baker sells 168 cream puffs a day. The cream puffs are sold 3 in a box. How many boxes of cream puffs can he sell in a week? (There are 7 days in a week.)

7. A crate contained 576 bottles of soda pop. The grocer gave half of them away during a promotion and sold the other half equally to 8 customers. How many bottles of soda pop did each customer buy?

8. Kumar has 216 cards. He has 9 times as many cards as Ashley. How many more picture cards does Kumar have than Ashley?

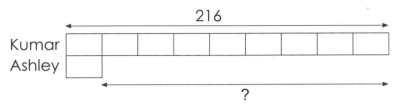

9. Bernard had 457 red marbles. His friend gave him 310 green marbles. He put all the marbles equally into 6 bags.
(a) How many marbles were there in one bag?
(b) How many marbles could not be put into a bag?

10. A storybook has 45 more pages than a magazine. If the storybook has 68 pages, how many pages does 7 similar magazines have?

Take the Challenge!

1. Put each of the digits from 1 to 9 in the empty spaces below to form correct number sentences across and down. Mathematical operations are to be carried out from left to right and from top to bottom.

?	×	?	−	?	= 3
×		−		−	
?	+	?	÷	?	= 3
−		×		+	
?	−	?	+	?	= 3
= 3		= 3		= 3	

56

2. A 4-digit number A B C D when multiplied by 4 gives another 4-digit number D C B A. What are the values of A, B, C and D? Each digit is different and it can be any number from 0 to 9.

$$
\begin{array}{r}
A \quad B \quad C \quad D \\
\times \qquad\qquad\quad 4 \\
\hline
D \quad C \quad B \quad A \\
\hline
\end{array}
$$

1. Write down the prices of the toys shown below.

$69.95 $9.25 $45.90 $29.45 $19.05 $22.75 $39.45 $0.90

(a) Rocking horse   – $69.95   ☐ dollars ☐ cents

(b) Small ball   – $0.90   ☐ dollars ☐ cents

(c) Rag doll   – $19.05   ☐ dollars ☐ cents

(d) Toy drum   – $22.75   ☐ dollars ☐ cents

(e) Large ball   – $9.25   ☐ dollars ☐ cents

(f) Toy rabbit   – $39.45   ☐ dollars ☐ cents

(g) Teddy bear   – $45.90   ☐ dollars ☐ cents

(h) Toy yacht   – $29.45   ☐ dollars ☐ cents

2. Write down the value of the money in each purse.

(a)

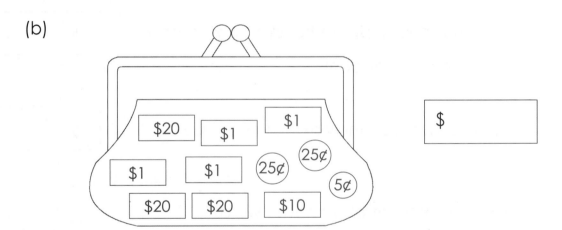

$ [   ]

(b)

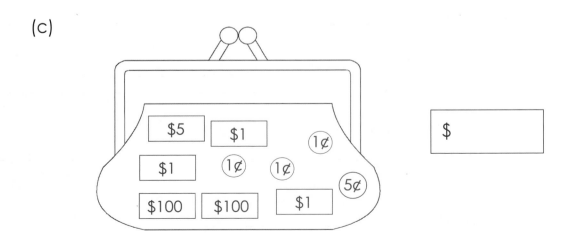

$ [   ]

(c)

$ [   ]

3. Write the amount of money in figures.

(a) Eight dollars and eighty-eight cents $\boxed{\$ \qquad}$

(b) Twenty dollars and nine cents $\boxed{\$ \qquad}$

(c) Sixty-four dollars and fifty-five cents $\boxed{\$ \qquad}$

(d) One hundred three dollars and six cents $\boxed{\$ \qquad}$

(e) One thousand, five hundred dollars and seventy-eight cents $\boxed{\$ \qquad}$

(f) Five hundred thirty-six dollars $\boxed{\$ \qquad}$

4. Write the amount of money in words.

(a) $0.91 _____

(b) $1.47 _____

(c) $12.05 _____

(d) $80.15 _____

(e) $607.00 _____

(f) $3402 _____

5. Fill in the correct number of the type of coins used to make up the amount of money given.

	Amount of money	Number of coins			
		nickel	dime	quarter	half-dollar
(a)	One dollar		10		2
(b)	Five dollars	100		20	
(c)	$0.60				
(d)	$1.50				
(e)	Ten dollars				

6. Complete the table with the value of the coins given.

	Coins used	Total value
(a)	8 dimes and 5 nickels	
(b)	4 quarters, 2 dimes, 11 nickels and 5 pennies	
(c)	22 pennies, 3 nickels, 10 dimes, and 5 quarters	
(d)	4 quarters and 20 nickels	
(e)	10 quarters and 4 dimes	

7. Express in dollars and cents or in cents.

(a) 5 ¢ $_____   (b) $0.35   _____ ¢

(c) 170 ¢ $_____   (d) $20.08   _____ ¢

(e) 3605 ¢ $_____   (f) $8.13   _____ ¢

(g) 8090 ¢ $_____   (h) $96.17   _____ ¢

8. Find the value of the following.

(a) $23.00 + $65.00 = _____

(b) $32.10 + $47.55 = _____

(c) $71.25 + $16.40 = _____

(d) $68.15 + $20.50 = _____

(e) $90.36 + $2.64 = _____

(f) $26.42 + $53.90 = _____

(g) $75.00 – $30.00 = _____

(h) $87.85 – $57.65 = _____

(i) $23.90 – $6.45 = _____

(j) $48.33 – $29.21 = _____

(k) $73.46 – $59.38 = _____

(l) $96.25 – $67.32 = _____

9. Work out these problems and unscramble the letters to find out who I am.

(a) $ 3.89
   + $ 12.75
 	
_____   **I**
	(b) $ 57.90
	   – $ 24.35
	
	_____ **Z**

(c) $56.12
   – $19.39
 	
_____   **M**
	(d) $79.18
	   + $16.43
	
	_____ **N**

(e) $68.94
   + $51.80
 	
_____   **B**
	(f) $ 100.00
	   – $ 37.65
	
	_____ **A**

_____   _____   _____   _____   _____   _____

$120.74 $16.64 $33.55 $36.73 $62.35 $95.61

WORD PROBLEMS

1. Complete the bill for the following items bought by Miss Jessie.

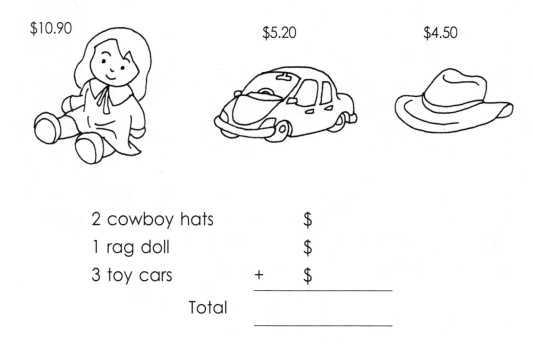

$10.90 $5.20 $4.50

2 cowboy hats		$
1 rag doll		$
3 toy cars	+	$
Total		

2. Betsy had $10.00. She bought a box of color pencils for $5.75. How much money does she have left?

3. Kim paid $23.80 for a tennis racket and had $44.00 left. How much money did she have at first?

4. Yasmin wanted to buy a skateboard which cost $79.87. She had only $51.99. How much money must she save in order to buy the skateboard?

5. Jamie received a gift of $100. She spent $55.99 on a pair of shorts and saved the rest. How much money did she save?

6. Anita had $98.50. She bought a dress for $86.90 and took a taxi home. She had $2.90 left. How much was the taxi fare?

7. Benjie went to the store with $92.10. He bought a jacket for $47.80. He then wanted to buy a coat for $55.50. How much more money did Benjie need to buy the coat?

8. Mrs. Lee bought a toy train and a construction set for her son. The toy train cost $33.90 while the construction set cost $29.00 more. How much did Mrs. Lee pay for the two toys?

9. Cindy saved $512.60. Holly saved $32.50 less than Cindy. Larry saved $48.30 more than Holly.
   (a) Who had the most savings?
   (b) How much was it?

10. Mr. Murray bought a shirt and a pair of trousers. He paid the cashier a $100 bill and received a change of $15.20. If the shirt cost $24.90, how much did the pair of trousers cost?

Take the Challenge!

1. Nancy has $14.15 and Joel has $29.85. How much must Joel give to Nancy so that both of them will have the same amount of money after that? (*Hint*: Is there any change in the total amount of money both have?)

2. Louise had exactly the amount of money to buy 8 similarly-priced video CDs. She changed her mind and bought only 5 video CDs. She found that she had $60 left.
   (a) What was the cost of 1 video CD?
   (b) If Louise bought 6 video CDs, how much would she have left?

3. 1 mango and 1 papaya together cost $4.70. Krystle bought 2 mangoes and 5 papayas for $13.00. How much did the 2 mangoes cost?

Mid-Year Review

PART 1

Work out the following problems and write the correct answer in the boxes provided.

1. Write 5065 in words.

2. In the numeral 8916, what does the digit '9' stand for?

3. Fill in the missing number in the pattern below.

    2685,   2695 ,   _____ ,   2715

4. What must you add to 5621 to get 8000?

5. The quotient of 512 and 8 is the same as  □ × □ .
   What is the missing number in each box if both are the same number?

6.  △ + ◇ + ⬠ = 10,000
   If △ = 3992 and ⬠ = 2047,

   find the value of ◇ .

7. What number comes next in the pattern below?

| 3250 | 3270 | 3300 | 3340 | |

8. _____ is 500 more than 3590 + 24.

9. There are _____ tens in 260 + 105.

10. What is the sum of 6 hundreds 7 ones and 3 thousands 2 tens?

11. The difference between the largest and the smallest of the numbers 1068, 793 and 2387 is _____ .

12. What number must be added to the difference between 512 and 343 to give a result of 200?

13. Study the patterns below and write the missing numbers.

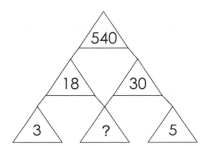
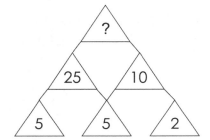

and

14. Fill in the missing numbers in the boxes.

```
  6 □ 3 8
- 3 7 7 9
_____
  2 2 □ 9
_____
```

15. What is the missing number in the box below?

$6 \times 9 = \boxed{} \div 3$

16. 200 more than 1830 is _____.

17. _____ is 250 less than 900.

18. Melissa has some money in her purse shown below. How much money does Melissa have altogether?

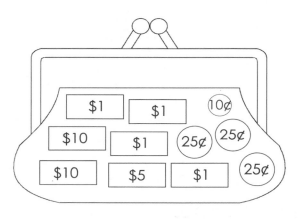

19. Study the number pattern below. What is the missing number?

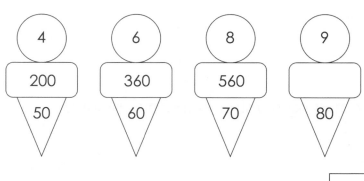

20. What is the number which when divided by 7 gives a quotient of 13 and a remainder of 4?

21. How many nines can be subtracted from 70?

nines

22. Find the difference between the largest even number and the smallest odd number that you can form using all of these digits.

23. If + + + stands for 32,

then + stands for _____.

24. The difference between two numbers is 264. What is the smaller number if the larger number is 1000?

25. Subtract 3899 from 9080. How many hundreds are there in the answer?

	hundreds

26. Which of the following shows the least amount of money?
    4 quarters
    $1.08
    100 pennies
    16 nickels

27. If 🙂 + 🙂 + 🙂 gives 36

    and ✚ × ✚ gives 36,

    what is the quotient of 🙂 and ✚?

28. A grocer packed 105 lollipops equally into 7 bags. How many lollipops were there in each bag?

	lollipops

29. Sharon has 892 stickers. Her friend, Nina, has half as many as she. How many stickers do both girls have in all?

	stickers

30. Cecilia bought a handbag and paid the cashier using two $100 bills. She received a change of $39.60. How much did the handbag cost?

$

31. Nathan collected 375 coins from other countries. Amos collected twice as many coins as Nathan. How many coins did Amos have?

coins

32. A brand watch is now on sale. Mr. Govinda wants to buy 4 such watches. How much does he need to pay?

Great Watch Sale
Usual Price: $299.00
Now: $99.00 less !

$

33. Byron saved $352. He saved $49 less than his older brother, Kenny. How much savings did the two brothers have altogether?

$

34. A crate contained 60 apples. A grocer threw away 5 rotten ones and packed the remaining apples in bags of 5. How many bags did he get?

	bags

35. Charles has 287 stamps. Paul has thee times as many stamps as Charles. How many stamps do Charles and Paul have altogether?

	stamps

36. What is the digit in the box?

```
      1  3  3  r4
6 ) 8  □  2
```


37. 7, 14, 21, 28, 35, _____, 49, 56
What is the missing number in the number pattern?

38. 10 boxes of the same type contain 250 crystal beads. How many crystal beads do 6 such boxes contain?

	beads

39. Zoe bought two Christmas gifts for exactly $38. Which two items below did she buy?

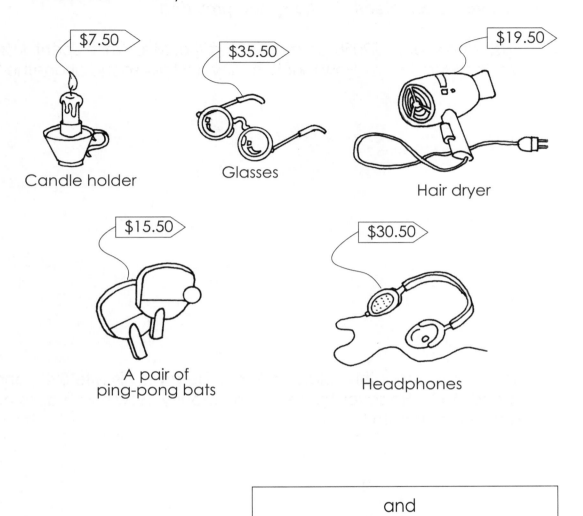

$7.50

Candle holder

$35.50

Glasses

$19.50

Hair dryer

$15.50

A pair of
ping-pong bats

$30.50

Headphones

	and	

40. Mr. Bean exchanged a 10-dollar bill for four $1 bills, twelve quarters and the remaining for dimes. How many dimes did he receive?

	dimes

PART 2

Show all your work clearly in the space provided.

41. Mrs. White spent $2058 on a shopping trip. Mrs. White spent $125 less than Mrs. Brown. How much money did they spend altogether?

42. Sam earns a monthly salary of $1800. He gives his wife $980 and spends $425. He saves the rest of the money. How much does he save every month?

43. An empty cardboard box and 6 cartons of milk packed into it weigh 6250 g. Find the weight of the empty cardboard box if each carton of milk weighs 925 g.

44. Harry placed 735 stamps equally into 8 albums.
    (a) How many stamps are there in 1 album?
    (b) How many stamps cannot be placed in an album?

45. Joseph has $55 savings. He wants to buy a baseball bat and some balls which cost $90 in total. If he saves $5 each week, how long will it take him to have enough money to buy the bat and balls?

46. A teacher brought 200 cookies and gave her class of 36 students each 4 cookies. She later gave some of the remaining cookies to the school janitor and had 12 left for herself. How many cookies did the janitor get?

47. Gerald bought 8 baseball gloves. He gave the cashier two $100 bills. He received a change of $8. What was the cost of each baseball glove?

48. (a) Mr. Nelson put up a fence at his backyard. He drove 10 wooden posts 120 cm apart into the ground. How long was the wooden fence?

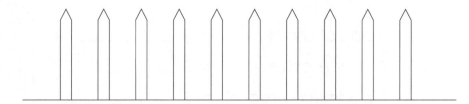

   (b) How many odd numbers are there between 301 and 321?

49. Below are the prices of the items that Davina bought at a departmental store. Complete her bill and work out her change when she paid the cashier $100.

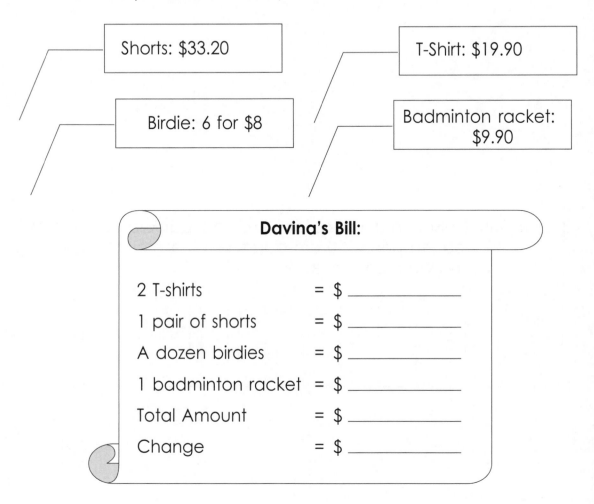

Shorts: $33.20

T-Shirt: $19.90

Birdie: 6 for $8

Badminton racket: $9.90

Davina's Bill:

2 T-shirts	= $ _____
1 pair of shorts	= $ _____
A dozen birdies	= $ _____
1 badminton racket	= $ _____
Total Amount	= $ _____
Change	= $ _____

50. Tania weighs 56 lb. Her father is 3 times as heavy as she. Her brother, Tom, is half as heavy as his father. How heavy is Tom?

More Challenging Problems

1. From the numbers 1 to 100,
   (a) how many times does the digit '1' appear?
   (b) how many times does the digit '0' appear?

2. What is the smallest possible answer for the following subtraction problem such that the boxes are to be filled by the numbers 2, 5, 7 and 9 (each number can only be used once)?

$$\boxed{}\ \boxed{}$$
$$-\ \boxed{}\ \boxed{}$$
$$\text{?}$$

85

3. In the following addition problem, what is A + B + C + D?

$$
\begin{array}{r}
\text{A B} \\
+ \quad \text{C D} \\
\hline
1 \ 4 \ 9
\end{array}
$$

4. Fill in the missing numbers in the boxes with numbers from 1 to 9. Each number can only be used once.

☐ + ☐ = ☐

☐ − ☐ = ☐

☐ × ☐ = ☐

5. Three cats take 3 minutes to eat a total of 3 fish at the same time. With this same rate, how long will it take 100 cats to eat a total of 100 fish at the same time?

6. Dawn needs to travel from Town A to Town C. If there are 4 routes from Town A to Town B and 5 routes from Town B to Town C, how many different routes can Dawn take from Town A to Town C?

7. At a tea-party, there were 100 people made up of men, women and children. Each man was given 3 sandwiches and each woman was given 2 sandwiches. As for the children, only 1 sandwich was shared between every 2 children. How many men, women and children were at the party if 100 sandwiches were shared among them?

8. Three numbers 1, 2 and 3, when added or multiplied together gives the same answer, 6. Four numbers 1, 1, 2 and 4, when added or multiplied together gives the same answer, 8. Can you find five numbers such that they will give the same answer when they are being added or multiplied together? List as many sets of these five numbers as possible.

9. There are 5 children sitting on a bench. In answering a question, each girl raises her right hand and each boy raises both his hands. If 8 hands are being raised altogether, how many girls are there?

10. There are 13 cards numbered from 1 to 13. Pick up three of these cards so that the numbers on these three cards when multiplied together gives 252.

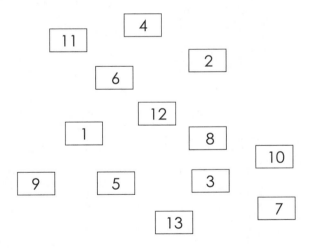

11. Three shapes ▢, ◯ and △ are arranged in a certain order as shown. If there are 100 shapes altogether in the pattern, how many are there for each shape?

▢◯◯◯△△△△△▢◯◯◯△△△△△▢◯ .....

Answers

Topic 1: Numbers to 10,000

1. (a) 9   (b) 4, 0
   (c) 5, 5   (d) 1, 8, 8
2. (a) 4   (b) 8923
   (c) 4   (d) 8
   (e) tens
3. (a) 8   (b) 40
   (c) 600   (d) 1000
   (e) 800   (f) 9000
4. (a) 500   (b) 600
   (c) 60   (d) tens
5. 900
6. (a) 6805   (b) 1089
   (c) 2801   (c) 6859, 3015
7. 2069, 2619, 2691, 2916
8. 8734, 8473, 7843, 7438
9. (a) 46   (b) 86   (c) 22
   (d) 800   (e) 6833   (f) 260
   (g) 30   (h) 6966   (i) 3794
   (j) 2654   (k) 5142   (l) 6
10. (a) 3688   (b) 7865
    (c) 1999   (d) 5380
11. (a) 8740   (b) 4078
    (c) 874   (d) 407
12. (a) 999   (b) 100   (c) 8999
    (d) 100   (e) 8999
13. (a) 99   (b) 10,000   (c) 899

Word Problems

1. $8600   2. 3892   3. 1188
4. 5780   5. $4155   6. 450
7. 276, 862   8. 199
9. (a) 34 large bags, 5 small bags
   (b) 7
10. 4580

Take the Challenge!

1. 126   2. 931   3. 100 m

Topic 2: Addition and Subtraction

1. *Across*
   (a) 3267   (b) 2735   (c) 4863
   (d) 5767   (e) 5041
   Down
   (c) 4522   (f) 6516   (g) 3373
   (h) 5019   (j) 7834

2. (a) 1881   (b) 4242   (c) 2154
   (d) 4811
3. 90   4. 52   5. 8410
6. 5841   7. 1849   8. 5514
9. (a) 7292   (b) 6901
   (c) 3729   (d) 5058
10. 680   11. 1406
12. 6614   13. 2492
14. (a) 3, 7   (b) 9, 0   (c) 0, 4
    (d) 5, 5   (e) 6, 5   (f) 9, 5
15. 8630   16. 1459   17. 400
18. 0   19. 1453   20. 150
21. 60   22. 1037   23. 988
24. 6001   25. 20   26. 700

Word Problems

1. 415   2. 332   3. 1240
4. (a) 9321, 1239   (b) 8082
5. 10 468   6. 532   7. 3738
8. (a) 3886   (b) 6022
9. 146   10. 1450

Take the Challenge!

1. 347, 256 or 357, 246; etc
2. 55
3. A = 0, E = 5, K = 1
4. A = 4, B = 7, C = 5, D = 3 is one solution.
   There are other solutions.

Topic 3: Multiplication and Division by 2, 3, 4, 5 and 10

1. (a) 12   (b) 14
   (c) 30   (d) 60
   (e) 28   (f) 45, 30, 35
   (g) 21, 27   (h) 32, 9, 28
2. (a) 6   (b) 40, 24
   (c) 2, 15   (d) 36, 45; 27, 18
3. (a) 4 × 5 = 20   (b) 45 ÷ 5 = 9
   (c) 3 × 9 = 27   (d) 36 ÷ 4 = 9
   (e) 5 × 10 = 50   (f) 35 ÷ 5 = 7
4. (a)

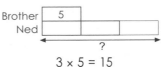

3 × 5 = 15

(b)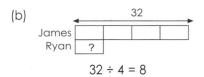
$$32 \div 4 = 8$$

(c)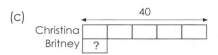
$$40 \div 5 = 8$$

(d)
$$7 \times 4 = 28$$

5. (a) 228   (b) 192   (c) 445
    (d) 500   (e) 1050   (f) 2800
    (g) 3752   (h) 1238   (i) 2295
    (j) 2768   (k) 1290   (l) 1227
6. (a) 27 r1   (b) 22 r1   (c) 51 r1
    (d) 22 r2   (e) 109 r1   (f) 132 r3
    (g) 94 r2   (h) 225 r0   (i) 119 r2
    (j) 161 r3   (k) 153 r2   (l) 225 r2
7. 45   8. 18   9. 59
10. 237   11. 144   12. 205
13. 168   14. 2415
15. 48, 52, 56, 61 ☒   16. 1
17. 182   18. 4   19. 40
20. (a) 6   (b) 3
21. (a) 2   (b) 9

Word Problems

1.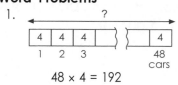
    $$48 \times 4 = 192$$

2.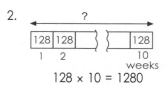
    $$128 \times 10 = 1280$$

3.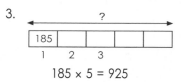
    $$185 \times 5 = 925$$

4.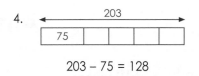
    $$203 - 75 = 128$$
    $$128 \div 4 = 32$$

5.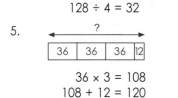
    $$36 \times 3 = 108$$
    $$108 + 12 = 120$$

6.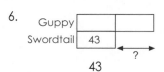
    43

7.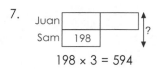
    $$198 \times 3 = 594$$

8.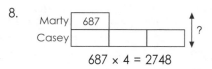
    $$687 \times 4 = 2748$$

9.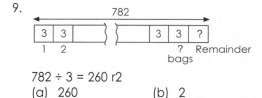
    $$782 \div 3 = 260 \text{ r2}$$
    (a) 260   (b) 2

10.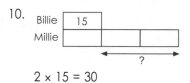
    $$2 \times 15 = 30$$

Take the Challenge!
1. 18
2. 6

Topic 4: Multiplication and Division by 6, 7, 8 and 9

1. (a) $6 \times 6 = 36$ and $36 \div 6 = 6$
    (b) $8 \times 6 = 48$ and $48 \div 8 = 6$
    (c) $5 \times 9 = 45$ and $45 \div 5 = 9$
    (d) $8 \times 7 = 56$ and $56 \div 7 = 8$

92

(e) $9 \times 8 = 72$ and $72 \div 8 = 9$
(f) $6 \times 9 = 54$ and $54 \div 9 = 6$
(g) $7 \times 9 = 63$ and $63 \div 7 = 9$
(h) $6 \times 7 = 42$ and $42 \div 7 = 6$

2. (a) 81, 7   (b) 64, 9   (c) 56, 54
   (d) 42   (e) 4, 18; 20, 4
3. (a) 742   (b) 1710   (c) 3136
   (d) 6183   (e) 2198   (f) 6000
   (g) 3564   (h) 2601   (i) 2910
   (j) 2264   (k) 4928   (l) 3681
4. (a) 14 r1   (b) 133 r3   (c) 63 r0
   (d) 75 r2   (e) 111 r7   (f) 94 r6
   (g) 66 r2   (h) 50 r4   (i) 57 r1
   (j) 129 r6   (k) 65 r4   (l) 124 r7
5. (a)

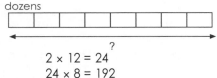

$2 \times 12 = 24$
$24 \times 8 = 192$

(b)

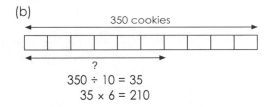

$350 \div 10 = 35$
$35 \times 6 = 210$

(c)

$352 \times 9 = 3168$
$3168 - 512 = 2656$

6. 14   7. 4
8. 21, 28, 35, 43 ✗   9. 1536
10. 742   11. 1640
12. 486   13. 7
14. (a) 4   (b) 8
15. (a) 5   (b) 6
16. (a) 288   (b) 300
17. 2401

Word Problems
1. 58   2. 350
3. (a) 23   (b) 230
4. 720   5. 2169
6. 392   7. 36
8. 192
9. (a) 127   (b) 5
10. 161

Take the Challenge!

1.

1	×	9	−	6	= 3
×		−		−	
7	+	8	÷	5	= 3
−		×		+	
4	−	3	+	2	= 3
= 3		= 3		= 3	

2. A can only be 1 or 2.
   A = 2, B = 1, C = 7, D = 8

Topic 5: Money

1. (a) 69, 95   (b) 0, 90   (c) 19, 5
   (d) 22, 75   (e) 9, 25   (f) 39, 45
   (g) 45, 90   (h) 29, 45
2. (a) $28.70   (b) $74.55   (c) $208.08
3. (a) $8.88   (b) $20.09   (c) $64.55
   (d) $103.06   (e) $1500.78   (f) $536.00
4. (a) Ninety-one cents
   (b) One dollar and forty-seven cents
   (c) Twelve dollars and five cents
   (d) Eighty dollars and fifteen cents
   (e) Six hundred seven dollars
   (f) Three thousand, four hundred two dollars
5. (a) 20, 4   (b) 50, 10   (c) 12, 6
   (d) 30, 15, 6, 3   (e) 40, 20
6. (a) $1.05   (b) $1.80   (c) $2.62
   (d) $2.00   (e) $2.90
7. (a) $0.05   (b) 35¢   (c) $1.70
   (d) 2008¢   (e) $36.05   (f) 813¢
   (g) $80.90   (h) 9617¢
8. (a) $88.00   (b) $79.65   (c) $87.65
   (d) $88.65   (e) $93.00   (f) $80.32
   (g) $45.00   (h) $30.20   (i) $17.45
   (j) $19.12   (k) $14.08   (l) $28.93
9. (a) $16.64   (b) $33.55   (c) $36.73
   (d) $95.61   (e) $120.74   (f) $62.35
   BIZMAN

Word Problems

1.
$$
\begin{array}{r}
\$\ 9.00 \\
\$10.90 \\
+\ \$15.60 \\
\hline
\$35.50
\end{array}
$$

2. $4.25
3. $67.80
4. $27.88
5. $44.01
6. $8.70
7. $11.20
8. $96.80
9. (a) Larry   (b) $528.40
10. $59.90

Take the Challenge!

1. $7.85
2. (a) $20   (b) $40
3. $7.00

Mid-Year Review

Part 1

1. Five thousand, sixty-five
2. 900
3. 2705   4. 2379
5. 8   6. 3961
7. 3390   8. 4114
9. 36   10. 3627
11. 1594   12. 31
13. 6, 250   14. 0, 5
15. 162   16. 2030
17. 650   18. $29.85
19. 720   20. 95
21. 7   22. 5661
23. 16   24. 736
25. 51   26. 16 nickels
27. 2   28. 15
29. 1338   30. $160.40
31. 750   32. $800.00
33. $753   34. 11
35. 1148   36. 0
37. 42   38. 150
39. Candle holder, Headphones
40. 30

Part 2

41. $4241   42. $395
43. 700 g
44. (a) 91   (b) 7
45. 7 weeks
46. 44   47. $24
48. (a) 1080 cm   (b) 9
49. $39.80, $33.20, $16.00, $9.90, $98.90, $1.10
50. 84 lb

More Challenging Problems

1. (a) 1, 10, 11, 12, 13, 14, 15, 16, 17, 18, 19, 21, 31, 41, 51, 61, 71, 81, 91, 100
   '1' appears 21 times.
   (b) 10, 20, 30, 40, 50, 60, 70, 80, 90, 100
   '0' appears 11 times.

2.
$$
\begin{array}{r}
7\ 2 \\
-\ \ 5\ 9 \\
\hline
1\ 3
\end{array}
$$

3. Since B + D cannot be 19, B + D must be 9.
   A + C = 14
   A + B + C + D = A + C + B + D
                 = 14 + 9
                 = 23

4. It is easier to start with the last number sentence as there are only 2 possible cases: 2 × 3 = 6 or 2 × 4 = 8.
   The possible solutions are:
4 + 5 = 9		7 + 1 = 8
8 − 7 = 1	or	9 − 5 = 4
2 × 3 = 6		2 × 3 = 6

5. 1 cat takes 3 minutes to eat 1 fish. 100 cats also take 3 minutes to eat a total of 100 fish.

6.

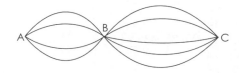

4 × 5 = 20 routes

7. 5 men: 5 × 3 = 15 pieces
   25 women: 25× 2 = 50 pieces
   70 children: 35 pieces

8. 1, 1, 1, 2, 5;
   1, 1, 1, 3, 3;
   1, 1, 2, 2, 2

9. There must be an even number of girls.
   2 girls : 2 × 1 hands = 2 hands
   3 boys : 3 × 2 hands = 6 hands
   There are 2 girls.

10.
2	252
2	126
3	63
3	21
7	7
	1

$252 = 2 \times 2 \times 3 \times 3 \times 7$
$ = 4 \times 9 \times 7$
The three cards are those numbered 4, 9 and 7.

11. The pattern forms groups of 9 shapes:
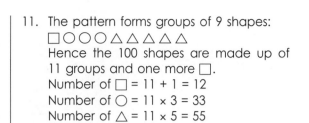
Hence the 100 shapes are made up of 11 groups and one more □.
Number of □ = 11 + 1 = 12
Number of ○ = 11 × 3 = 33
Number of △ = 11 × 5 = 55